WHO EATS

IN A CAGE?

A CAGED

OR WITH

MOUTH?

AHSAHTA PRESS
BOISE, IDAHO
2015

THE NEW SERIES

#67

ANNE BOYER

GARMENTS AGAINST WOMEN

Ahsahta Press, Boise State University, Boise, Idaho 83725-1525
ahsahtapress.org
Cover design by Quemadura / Book design by Janet Holmes

LIBRARY OF CONGRESS CATALOGING-IN-PUBLICATION DATA
Boyer, Anne, 1973-
[Prose works. Selections]
Garments against women / Anne Boyer.
pages ; cm—(The new series ; #67)
ISBN 978-1-934103-59-3 (acid-free paper)
I. Title.
PS3602.O935A6 2015
818'.6—dc23
                            2014045278

Notes and acknowledgments appear on page 89.

"The books she had obtained, were soon devoured, by one who had no other resource to escape from sorrow, and the feverish dreams of ideal wretchedness or felicity, which equally weaken the intoxicated sensibility. Writing was then the only alternative, and she wrote some rhapsodies descriptive of the state of her mind; but the events of her past life pressing on her, she resolved circumstantially to relate them, with the sentiments that experience, and more matured reason, would naturally suggest. They might perhaps instruct her daughter, and shield her from the misery, the tyranny, her mother knew not how to avoid."

MARY WOLLSTONECRAFT
FROM *MARIA: OR, THE WRONGS OF WOMAN*

CONTENTS

THE ANIMAL MODEL OF INESCAPABLE SHOCK

If an animal has previously suffered escapable shock, and then she suffers inescapable shock, she will be happier than if she has previously not suffered escapable shock—for if she hasn't, she will only know about being shocked inescapably. But if she has been inescapably shocked before, and she meets the conditions in which she was inescapably shocked before, she will behave as if being shocked, mostly. Her misery doesn't require acts. Her misery requires conditions.

If an animal is inescapably shocked once, then the second time that she is shocked she is dragged across the electrified grid to some non-shocking space, she will be happier than if she isn't dragged across the electrified grid. The next time she is shocked, she will be happier because she will know there is a place that isn't an electrified grid. She will be happier because rather than only being dragged onto an electrified grid by a human who then hurts her, the human can also then drag her off of it.

If an animal is shocked, escapably or inescapably, she will manifest deep attachment for whoever has shocked her. If she has manifested deep attachment for whoever has shocked her, she will manifest deeper reactions of attachment for whoever has shocked her and then dragged her off the electrified grid. Perhaps she will develop deep feelings of attachment for electrified grids. Perhaps she will develop deep feelings of attachment for what is not the electrified grid. Perhaps she will develop deep feelings of attachment for dragging. She may also develop deep feelings of attachment for science, laboratories, experimentation, electricity, and informative forms of torture.

If an animal is shocked, her body will produce an analgesic. This will involve endogenous opioids. This will be better than anything. Later, there will be no opioids, and she will go back to who and what has shocked her looking for more. She will go to the shocking condition—"science"—and there in this condition she will flood with endogenous opioids, along with cortisol and other arousing inner substances.

Eventually all arousal will feel like shock. She will not be steady, though, in her self-supply of analgesic. She will not always be able to dwell in science, as much as she now believes she loves it.

That humans are animals means it is possible that the animal model of inescapable shock explains why humans go to movies, lovers stay with those who don't love them, the poor serve the rich, the soldiers continue to fight, and other confused, arousing things. Also, how is Capital not an infinite laboratory called "conditions"? And where is the edge of the electrified grid?

THE INNOCENT QUESTION

Some of us write because there are problems to be solved. Sometimes there are specific, smaller problems. A friend who has a job as a telephone transcriptionist for people who can't hear has had to face the problem of what to do when one party he is transcribing has sobbed.

(He puts the sobs in parentheses.)

This is the problem of what-to-do-with-the-information-that-is-feeling.

Another friend (a poet) writes poems with many words in parentheses. I dream he sends me an email which is a survey requesting information. I respond to his survey, and when I do, the information becomes a three-dimensional topographical map. The map is both like a bowl and like America, and on it my information has been turned into states of many colors, most shaped like Colorado, some like West Virginia. The information I provided was my feelings, so there is grief in my dreams, square, red, and with a cluster of mountains rising from it.

I think of all those things conferring authority and exclude them one by one, an experiment in erasing importance. I thought there would be no better game to play than the game set up already, the game called "voice in the crowd of voices." I didn't mark a piece of paper the whole month long.

I'll remove this thing, but in doing so make it legitimate. I'm an ordinary human who likes objects, too. This is the opposite of how life goes, its steady progression of scars and accolades.

Monuments are interesting mostly in how they diminish all other aspects of the landscape. Each highly perceptible thing makes something else almost imperceptible. This is so matter of fact, but I've been told I'm incomprehensible: *Anne, what do you mean that noticing one thing can make the other things disappear?*

At first, I meant to write a treatise on happiness, but only as a kind of anti-history. This morning the impulse was to read every book. I was cleaved apart by invisible axes, crumbling, full of nausea, stinking of biology with 980 pounds tied to each limb. That's an awkward way to do one's work. Charlie made a drawing for the magazine: *less typing, more touching.* I feel like I read some, but still there are so many things of such importance about which I have never found a book.

I wanted to be really ordinary like an animal. I thought it was my writing that was making me sick. When I was writing I had many symptoms including back spasms and ocular migraines, and then when I was not writing I spent one month feverish, infected in many places, weak, coughing, voiceless, allergic, itchy, with swollen joints, hands, and feet. Finally there was something that almost cured me. The thing that almost cured me was a touch of Frost & Glow in my hair on top of a cocktail of Zyrtec, Zantac, Claritin, Benadryl, Singulair, Zithromax, Vicodin, Advil, Yaz, Retin A, and Albuteral. The Frost & Glow, not frosted at all but painted onto the tips of the lower layer of my hair, had restorative effects, as if the smallest bit of drugstore blonde could alter a person's person so that she would no longer be anxious and beleaguered and prone to many infections and tragedies and immune system over-reactions to the deep terrible of survival but would soon be wearing a fitted orange sundress with pink flowers printed on it and playing pool in a suburban bar and grill.

The accountant and the air-conditioning repair man then said "Look at that sexy mouth. Look at those sexy legs" as if erased from the page of the body they were reading was that only hours before (before the Frost & Glow) that mouth and those legs were part of a story that read exactly as it was, told in the throes.

I mean that things changed after the Frost & Glow. Things change.

Some people believe to know the fin is to know a shark, but this is an incorrect belief. The fin is not a fin of a shark at all though it is a reproduction shark fin strapped on a boy's back, and the boy with the reproduction fin does very much want to be a shark, wishes it a great deal, dreams some nights of being a shark in a great fleet of sharks in some unexplored sea where sharks are in fleets and somewhat even more powerful that the sharks of the daytime world have shark banks full of money and minnows. One could be, also, a person with a fabulous malformation of a shark fin on her back, who says often "please excuse the fin" but others look at it and say, "look at that grand shark with that awesome fin" when she is, underneath the fin, a person who is fond of peeling carrots for soup and a person who could otherwise just not help the fin that fortune dealt her. Some could be real sharks, the fin an adequate representation of sharkly reality: that's just the deal.

I live in the innocent question. Subjectivity will be convulsive. I read on the Internet these words about art, philosophy, politics, and poetry, also this information about the lives of my friends.

Inadmissible information is often information that has something to do with biology (illness, sex, reproduction) or money (poverty) or violence (how money and bodies meet). Inadmissible information might also have to do with being defanged by power (courts, bosses, fathers, editors, and other authorities) or behaving against power in such a way that one soon will be defanged (crime).

Often what is perceived by one party to be an over-reaction to circumstances is the case of that one party not having sufficient information because the information being reacted to is the inadmissible information of the other.

To feel deeply, or to admit to feeling deeply, is also inadmissible, though not as inadmissible as to admit to having been un-free.

Inadmissible information is inadmissible because it provokes a kind of social discomfort, like how if a group of poor people are in the room with one not-poor person the poor people might without conferring about it work together to carefully conceal their own poverty for the benefit of the other, not-poor person, sometimes going so far as to increase their poverty by paying for the things they cannot afford.

Many kinds of inadmissible information are inadmissible because they provoke a feeling of pity, guilt, or contempt. All three of these (pity, guilt, and contempt) are feelings of power, are the emotional indulgences of those with power or those who seek it. Who wants to admit the information that will make more wealthy those already so ugly with being rich?

For a month I had wondered what happiness was, then I found a book on happiness from a thrift store (*The Strategies and Tactics of Happiness Volume 1: Background* by Maynard W. Shelly). It had chapters with titles like "Having Everything is Wonderful" and "Missing a Few Things is Great." Shelly argues that happiness is about having enough resources, but not too many. He makes no arguments for happiness or against it. This book, which was printed in soft ink in 1977, has hand drawings of happy or sad figures and these marvelous looking subtitles which are set in all caps as if they are being shouted. These are subtitles like

THE RICHNESS OF UNPLEASANT SETTINGS AND THE RICHNESS OF UNPLEASANT MIND EVENTS BOTH TEND TO INCREASE WITH TIME WHEN SUCH SETTING OR SUCH EVENTS CANNOT BE AVOIDED

or

THE MORE INTENSE THE ANTICIPATED SATISFACTION ASSOCI-ATED WITH A GOAL, THE MORE MEDIATED SATISFACTIONS IT WILL GENERATE AND THE MORE IT WILL ORGANIZE SATISFAC-TION SEEKING

I thought I, too, would write about happiness if I were ever to write again. For who better to consider sleep than the insomniac?[1] But as I became very ill, I thought less about happiness and had instead many thoughts like "I do not want to be ill" and "It is difficult to work with

---

[1] "A man who falls straight into bed night after night, and ceases to live until the morning when he wakes and rises, will surely never dream of making, I don't say great discoveries, but even minor observations about sleep. He scarcely knows that he is asleep."

a high fever" and "I wish someone were here to take care of me" and "How will I pay to see a doctor?" Then I applied Frost & Glow to my hair, became almost well, and decided that happiness is a temporary state achieved in those days or weeks after one has been very ill and is not that ill anymore. It was in this brief period that I could hold a visceral memory of having been miserable firmly enough to appreciate almost being sick no more that I experienced something like happiness. I dressed a young man in a leopard fur coat and sent him walking through the neighborhoods like that. There was a rising interest in tango dancing. I allowed myself to eat liberal amounts of fresh fruit. I had some words in my head, rather some phrases, like "as the flea goes we go and pick up that grief" and "steam boats spring" and "the frontier is soily."

I decided I could read something other than Rousseau. Though I was experiencing this often truant condition, happiness, this did not mean that my mind was behaving admirably. Wasn't it stupid to take pleasure in the fact of being sort of well? I was happy but stupid or least more stupid than usual. And happiness had always seemed the province of the idiotic and immoral, which is why I wanted it so-much so-often so-all-of-the-time. There are many things I do not like to read, mostly accounts of the lives of the free.

Maynard Shelly wrote something about how life without sufficient constraints produces aimlessness, alienation, and boredom. So it is that the constrainingly unconstrained literature of Capital produced aimlessness, alienation, and boredom in me when I try to read it. I am now constrained to abundance, "happiness" or its absence / infirmity.

I get spam from Versailles. It seems like all my life I have gotten images of hard-ons in the mail. What is the difference between happiness and pornography? I mean what is the difference between literature and photography? It would be easy at first to confuse that which makes us happy and that which makes us aroused. It would be easy at first to confuse documentation and duplication. What I like on this earth is the company of bright young men. I am not a fan of infirmity, though it does supply the opportunity for some relief. It is all this self-expression that makes me so ashamed. In the comment boxes of a popular fashion blog someone suggested any documentation of individual expression is in fact anti-social rather than pro-social, in that it is a record of individuation from the human mass. There are those who hate the expression of any self that is not their own or like their own. They do not find happiness in the fact that day after day women and men take photos of themselves wearing clothes, never the same outfit twice. Maynard Shelly wrote something like

CREATIVE POWER IS THE CREATIVE ASPECT OF POWER REFLECT-
ING OUR ABILITY TO CREATE PSYCHOLOGICAL RESOURCES IN
SPACE

Other things that cause discomfort: people picking through the trash for their food. There are those who want "only the best" and those who believe only-the-best is immoral. I would talk about these two impulses, one for comfort, the other for justice, and how one appears animal, the other not that animal at all, for what dog says of her litter, "It is not only my own that should have my milk, but I will suckle the world"? I would like to meet that dog. I am the dog who can never be happy because I am imagining the unhappiness of other dogs.

There are the trash eaters: there are the diamond eaters. The diamond eaters are biblical; the trash eaters only so much in that they are lepers. I am on the side of the trash eaters, though I have eaten so many diamonds they are now poking through my skin. Everyone tries to figure out how to overcome the embarrassment of existing. We embarrass each other with comfort and justice, happiness or infirmity. It is embarrassing to be pornography; it is embarrassing to not be pornography. That requires a succor like limitation. Let's be happy insofar as we were for a few days not infirm. Happiness is only the absence of some ailment, but arousal is a source of unhappiness: I am writing to you in a long paragraph so that I will not be pornography. If you read this you will not be turned on.

"The classic example of positive contrast is produced by hitting yourself on the head with a hammer. The pain produced is part of the ordered dimension and so the more of it the more you get adapted to. Thus, when you stop you 'feel great.'"

I didn't intend for this to be an invitation. In the kitchen I was chopping vegetables and thinking about how discourse is a conspiracy, then how discourse is a conspiracy like "taste," then how taste is a weapon of class. Those guys have gotten together and agreed on their discourse; it will make them seem middling, casual like a sweater. Who dips in or out of it? What does it mean to give stuff up? There is a risk inherent in sliding all over the place. As if the language of poets is the language of property owners. As if the language of poets is the language of professors. As if the language of poets is not the language of machines. I would prefer to have a different name, that way in the strip malls I could be someone other than what I know and don't know about language. What does this have to do with happiness? "Let me fortify myself against death."

I think mostly about clothes, sex, food, and seasonal variations. I have done so much to be ordinary and made a record of this: first I was born, next I was a child, then I learned things and did things and loved and had those who loved me and often felt alone. My body was sometimes well, then sometimes unwell. I got nearer to death, as did you.

This is an exercise in numbers. This is against information. On the local radio show a man who won a Pulitzer prize in fiction explained that one must write every day because if a person does not write everyday a person forgets how to access the subconscious. If one did not write everyday then whenever a person comes back to writing she would have to learn to write from the beginning again. This has always been my plan. I would like to not know how to write, also to know no words. I believe this prize winning novelist believed that the mind had two places, the conscious and subconscious, and that literature could only come out of the subconscious mind, but that language preferred to live in the conscious one. This is wrong. Language prefers to live on the Internet.

I left off here. People came back. There was talking and art and talking about art and food and drink and food and more people who came back. I thought *everyone around me is noisy and they are saying "oatmeal" "toast" "cheese" "ice cream" and "sausage" and "it is good" and "that is not what I had in mind when I said toast."*

Maynard Shelly has a chapter (Chapter 12): THESE THINGS PRODUCE EXCITEMENTS AND TENSIONS. He includes incompleteness, concurrent incompleteness, ambiguity, and incongruity.

"showing the sculptured head of a chimp to a chimp who has never seen a piece of sculpture before will induce so much arousal that the chimp will go into a panic"

Good to keep counting to ward this stuff off. No one needs "————" And after math

it has altogether ceased to be practical to own *things* in the months of January and August. Strange *thing* to insist that we own.

little song   "if middle class
little song   "free from the defining institutions of the cities which them-
                selves define
little song   "then late art was an embrace of late capital now late poetry
                was an embrace of late art

We're good—cheering content providers, boring despots—with a note-book in which to record the history of our stockpile of foods:

history dwindles.

The anarchist pop star had a baby with the billionaire's son. It's a green gray blur of guns and money. It was proof for those who needed it that she didn't really mean what she said.

The syntactical evidence of poetry without the frame of poetry is a crime that is much more criminal. Or rather, if it is not in the frame of poetry, poetic syntax is evidence, mostly, of having no sense.

There'd be no Artaud here. Or rather, there is only Artaud, but not on these islands. There were seas (and these were rabid seas). There were islands (and these arose from the rabid seas). There were certain conventions at these times: to fly, to conference, to panel, to anthologize. In other circles it was to contest, submit, or award. I'd never been granted anything. I was perfectly willing to assign to my own refusal some sort of pathology. I was already sick, so what would I retrieve?

Poetry was the wrong art for people who love justice. It was not like dance music. Painting is the wrong art for people who love justice. It is not like science fiction. Epics are the dance music of the people who love war. Movies are the justice of the people who love war. Information is the poetry of the people who love war.

You should know this: that feed is your poem.

We get only slivers of the self-directed life. At first, a pie chart, then something else: there is a brute in these rooms and apartments and duplexes and trailers and shared houses and single-family houses and estates. The brute is not human, but like a bear, if a bear were a shadow and ten times bigger than a bear. This brute like a shadow and a bear not a human is named *survival-life*. The brute is always saying something, is saying give me the labor of your body, not the work of your hands. We fall asleep in that bear's arms.

My favorite arts are the ones that can move your body or make a new world. What at first kept me enthralled wasn't justice, it was justice-like waves, and a set of personal issues, like the aestheticization of politics and the limitations of reading lists before the digital age.

In conclusion, there would be no army of clay soldiers in the tomb, just this: an army of dress forms.

There is no superiority in making things or in re-making things. It's like everything else, old men who go fishing, hair extensions, nail art, individual false eyelashes glued on with semi-permanent glue, sewing clothes and re-sewing clothes, sketching, sketching animals, sketching human faces, sketching flowers, growing flowers, flowers, flowers that might even be marigolds and petunias, perfume that smells like party girls, perfume that smells like dowagers, perfume that does not smell like flowers or more like flowers mixed with the urine of jungle animals and some tobacco smoke, perfume that does not smell like men, one faux-Chanel earring, sunglasses resembling those of RAF leader Ulrike Meinhof, hair pinned up on one side, purses that are not real, pockets on dresses and skirts, dresses and skirts, blouses without buttons, limiting each type of possession to one old suitcase full of that type of possession, track suits with rhinestones, zip up onesie track suits, plump women, fat children, fat dogs, slender men, photos of Angelica Houston, the cracked dirty swimming pools of low-rent apartment complexes, bleach-haired boys smoking dope against the chain-link fence, the workers walking to their strip mall jobs, the strip malls, the dumpsters behind the strip malls, the karaoke nights in the bars in the strip malls, physique training, hypertrophy, very heavy weights, Juicy Stacey, Toy Selectah, every apartment complex having its own ducks, waking each spring morning to those ducks, the stateless state of contract labor, the invisible iv also the invisible catheter, everyone hugging the duct tape replica like starving little rhesus monkeys,

everything in the everything like "there is no world but the world!"

AT LEAST TWO TYPES OF PEOPLE

There are at least two types of people, the first for whom the ordinary worldliness is easy. The regular social routines and material cares are nothing too external to them and easily absorbed. They are not alien from the creation and maintenance of the world, and the world does not treat them as alien. And also, from them, the efforts toward the world, and to them, the fulfillment of the world's moderate desires, flow. They are effortless at eating, moving, arranging their arms as they sit or stand, being hired, being paid, cleaning up, spending, playing, mating. They are in an ease and comfort. The world is for the world and for them.

Then there are those over whom the events and opportunities of the everyday world wash over. There is rarely, in this second type, any easy kind of absorption. There is only a visible evidence of having been made of a different substance, one that repels. Also, from them, it is almost impossible to give to the world what it will welcome or reward. For how does this second type hold their arms? Across their chest? Behind their back? And how do they find food to eat and then prepare this food? And how do they receive a check or endorse it? And what also of the difficulties of love or being loved, its expansiveness, the way it is used for markets and indentured moods?

And what is this second substance? And how does it come to have as one of its qualities the resistance of the world as it is? And also, what is the person made of the second substance? Is this a human or more or less than one? Where is the true impermeable community of the second human whose arms do not easily arrange themselves and for whom the salaries and weddings and garages do not come?

These are, perhaps, not two sorts of persons, but two kinds of fortune. The first is soft and regular. The second is a baffled kind, and magnetic only to the second substance, and made itself out of a different, second, substance, and having, at its end, a second, and almost blank-faced, reward.

SEWING

Having given up literature, it was easy to become fixed on the idea of a single shirt, one with two pieces, no facings, not even set-in sleeves.

What can be done? How can two flat pieces joined together in four places accommodate a grown woman's torso, not at all flat, and with arms often in motion? It's just the same thing over and over, like when I used to listen to music, always stuck on a track, just this time in flannel, that time in linen, so many double pointed darts around the waistline cinching it in (Platonic ideal).

Every morning I wake up with a renewed commitment to learning to be what I am not. This is the day in which I will sew a straight seam, cut a piece of fabric precisely, follow the directions written by the pattern maker: stay stitch, clip notches. I will not presume to know more than the experts. I will always iron. No more jumping ahead, rebellion, daydreaming.

Each morning here is that sting of self-doubt, the chances of a wearable garment slim.

There are a lot of sleepless nights over seam finishes. In the heat of things, full of passionate expectation, I do things abruptly, crudely, mowing down the right-side-together ⅝ " , eager to see what is flat turn into what has shape. Then regret—with a little planning, that could have been a French seam, or something better, exotic or sturdy or spectacularly imitative of ready-to-wear. The sewing book says the quality of one's seam is really the measure of one's character. That gets repeated a lot. That's bad news. I think of some future for the garment, inspected in the thrift store where it will someday rest: *this was not an attentive sewist,* the future shopper thinks, and wrinkles her nose or whatever, shrugs. It's me always praying no one will ever look at the inside of my blue skirt. To never leave evidence of excitement (someday, soon, finally).

At the Salvation Army I bought a gray silk polka-dotted wrap dress made a very long time ago by a woman named Louise Jones. She sewed a "fashioned by Louise Jones" label inside the neck of it. She gave it fine French seams. I bought that dress for four dollars along with a wide gold belt to wear with it for one dollar. The dress smells like lotion, or rather like old lotion and the smell of a body which must be the odor of the extraordinary seamstress Louise Jones.

It's really not better to imitate ready-to-wear. Louise Jones seemed to know this. People who don't sew don't know this. My daughter brings me some knitwear: *but can you do that*? She's pointing to a double-stitched finishing. Yeah, I say, I have double needle, but that doesn't mean I want to use it, not now. There's also that problem of people who think things are always better if done by machine. I mean, so did I, so guilty, really, thinking badly of hand-picked zippers. I could spend a year learning to do well what I have spent twenty years doing badly, and after that year, I could still be bad at what I do.

One of the inventors of the sewing machine didn't patent it because of the way it would restructure labor. Another was almost killed by a mob.

Always when I sew I think of Emma Goldman with her sewing machine, or Emma Goldman during her first night in jail "at least bring me some sewing." Wikipedia says the sewing machine reduced average garment construction time from 14 hours to 2 hours. Somewhere on a sewing blog someone wrote of making new garments from existing ones: "use every part of the garment" and "each garment holds in it hours of a garment worker's life." I sew and the historical of sewing becomes a feeling just as when I used to be a poet, when I used to write poetry, used to write poetry and that thing—culture—began tendriling out in me, but it is probably more meaningful to sew a dress than to write a poem. I make anywhere from 10 to 15 dollars an hour at any of my three jobs. A garment from Target or Forever 21 costs 10 to 30 dollars. A garment from a thrift store costs somewhere between 4 and 10 dollars. A garment at a garage sale costs 1 to 5 dollars. A garment from a department store costs 30 to 500 dollars. All of these have been made, for the most part, from hours of women and children's lives. Now I give the hours of my life I don't sell to my employers to the garments. My costs are low: 2-dollar fabric from Goodwill, patterns bought for 99 cents or less, notions found at estate sales for 1 or 3 dollars. I almost save money like this. The fabric still contains the hours of the lives, those of the farmers and shepherds and chemists and factory workers and truckers and salespeople and the first purchasers, the givers-away, who were probably women who sewed. Sewing is difficult. There is a reason girls were trained in it before they were trained in anything else, years and years spent at practice, and even then they might not have been any good.

Sometimes when you look at smoothly joining at least two different-sized pieces of flat but pliable material so that these pieces might correctly encase an eternally irregular, perspiring and breathing three-dimensional object that cannot cease its motion you think that there is no way ever this could happen, yet sometimes it does.

Even heroic refusals often aren't that heroic though some are more heroic than others.

The best garment made out of a scarf is the skirt made of two scarves one of the sex workers wears in *Le Notti di Cabiria*. She's the angry one who is getting older who has the hard face and hard bangs shouting at Cabiria that Cabiria, too, will get old and beg someday. Cabiria only really gets pissed off and stops dancing at the mention of Giorgio. This sex worker has, like many of the sex workers in the movie, garments and accessories made of the pelts of animals or made of fibers that resemble these pelts. Cabiria herself often looks like a drowned cat in her fur or fur-like jacket. I not so long ago found a rabbit-hair sweater printed in the pattern of a snake skin and bought at the same time to wear with it a leopard-printed belt.

I set in sleeves. Perfected the skirt. Made one bright blue cord A-line skirt, one brown twill narrow skirt, one blue narrow skirt (no yoke), one brown linen top with dolman sleeves and three mother-of-pearl buttons, one brown twill top with a black yoke, one black wrap top from a vintage pattern. Learned the key to everything was not the time spent on the machine but the time spent with a needle in hand.

I'm okay with subjectivity. It's silky wovens that mess me up. I put everything back in its place, thinking I ought to be sewing less and writing more. Everyday I have a list called "Everyday."

It's only necessary to make a transparent account if it's necessary to have accounting, and it's only necessary to have accounting in the service of a profitable outcome. To account in the service of profit is to assume the desirability of profit. The individual doing the accounting is, like who or what she serves, also assumed to be in the service of profit, as profit is assumed to be desirable, and if she is in the service of profit, it's assumed she would like to profit also, and that what she would do if there were no transparency is cause herself to profit.

Without an open book, she would, following her assumed desire, steal, so that she makes a transparent account is always first in some service of that larger body that is the order of business. If she makes a transparent account, she may or should profit in one only one way: to benefit, as a reward for service to the order of business, and from the profitability of the larger body, and benefit, likewise, from behaving as a small replication of the order of business herself.

She is accounting transparently because there is a larger body which claims to know her heart: it assumes her heart is naturally a heart desiring profit, a heart which reflects (in miniature) the fundamental desire of the larger body, too. Or perhaps this is her heart or perhaps she has been convinced that to keep a clear and open record will be to be her benefit. Or, if she is not convinced this is to her benefit, she has been convinced she has no choice but to act in accord. She has been convinced that this is what one does when one has nothing to hide.

Yet this is not "nothing to hide": it is "something to show"—a performance, for the order of business, that her desires are in accord with its, that she would so naturally desire profit as to want to steal it and therefore, her "something to show" is the naturalness of the larger body's desires.

The accounting is also the transparency required, by convention, among humans in human relationships like children to their parents, of a husband to his wife, or a friend to a friend. It could be the transparent account of oneself and one's life required by those service jobs—so many—which require of their workers "the best intentions" and an "open heart." It could also be a "transparent account" that is literature.

If the books are muddled, confused, lost, damaged, inconsistent or otherwise opaque, the bookkeeper has provided a suspect record. She has probably stolen. Or maybe not. But the proof of her bad deed is in the presentation of opaqueness, and the heart's alignment with the one desire is, by the larger body, assumed. And maybe she has. To steal is to behave as a natural extension and reinforcement of a desire that everyone knows is what's real.

It's a requirement of the idea of the "transparent account" that someone should steal as an affirmation of the desirability of profit. It is like how marriage requires adultery, or journalism requires poets, or how the family requires that children will sometimes run away.

But maybe the person has thought about accounting, and thought about how it gives the wrong forms to desire insofar as the very act of it is to give reinforcement to a very limited one, has thought maybe there's a greater crime than embezzlement, and this is the refusal of accounting altogether. And what, this person asks, about how a transparent account is not actually anything like veracity, how there is another veracity that includes conspiracy, corners, shadows, slantwise, evasion, unsayingness, negation, and under-the-beds?

She might just prefer to be neither bookkeeper nor embezzler finally, when desire with an audience becomes, like pornography, a desire about the audience's desires, and there is another desire: to keep one's desire for one's self and off the books.

To refuse a bookkeeperly transparency is to protect the multiplicity of what we really want. Like the body's books, like the public's records, literature is just left there, open, as if its openness, its transparency—the "anybodiness" of its reader—is anything like the truth. But in conspiracy, verity.

THE VIRUS READER

I offered his virus to the mechanized virus reader. It had many functions, among these the one that translated "virus" into "sick room architectures." Thus the design specs for his recovery: a 15′ × 15′ outdoor room with a perimeter of medium-height pines, inside of these pines a hospital bed and an eight-foot flat-screen TV.

"at first it appeared that she was weeping so that I might change my mind and buy the $44 shoes, but soon she was unable to stop weeping. she refused to try on other shoes in other stores even though the shoes she wore were too small and had recently been in a mud puddle. she could see how even not-the-best-shoes-ever not-the-shoes-that-looked-like-art would be better than dirty ill-fitting shoes, but she could not stop weeping. we walked through stores while she wept. we sat in the middle of the mall while she wept. we went to a discount store, and I told her I would just pick out shoes for her because she wept too much to try on shoes. she wept in the discount store. she wasn't weeping by design. she couldn't stop weeping, then she stopped weeping a little and we found some brown sneakers for $44 on clearance. in the car I wanted to weep, too, but she said to me 'I am still a child and am learning to control my impulses and emotions. you have had many years of dreams and realities to learn from so there is no excuse for you to cry.' she paused. 'do you have enough dreams?' she finally asked."

NOT WRITING

When I am not writing I am not writing a novel called *1994* about a young woman in an office park in a provincial town who has a job cutting and pasting time. I am not writing a novel called *Nero* about the world's richest art star in space. I am not writing a book called *Kansas City Spleen*. I am not writing a sequel to *Kansas City Spleen* called *Bitch's Maldoror*. I am not writing a book of political philosophy called *Questions for Poets*. I am not writing a scandalous memoir. I am not writing a pathetic memoir. I am not writing a memoir about poetry or love. I am not writing a memoir about poverty, debt collection, or bankruptcy. I am not writing about family court. I am not writing a memoir because memoirs are for property owners and not writing a memoir about prohibitions of memoirs.

When I am not writing a memoir I am also not writing any kind of poetry, not prose poems contemporary or otherwise, not poems made of fragments, not tightened and compressed poems, not loosened and conversational poems, not conceptual poems, not virtuosic poems employing many different types of euphonious devices, not poems with epiphanies and not poems without, not documentary poems about recent political moments, not poems heavy with allusions to critical theory and popular song.

I am not writing "Leaving the Atocha Station" by Anne Boyer and certainly not writing "Nadja" by Anne Boyer though would like to write "Debt" by Anne Boyer though am not writing also "The German Ideology" by Anne Boyer and not writing a screenplay called "Sparticists."

I am not writing an account of myself more miserable than Rousseau. I am not writing an account of myself more innocent than Blake.

I am not writing epic poetry although I like what Milton said about lyric poets drinking wine while epic poets should drink water from a wooden bowl. I would like to drink wine from a wooden bowl or to drink water from an emptied bottle of wine.

I am not writing a book about shopping, which is a woman shopping.
I am not writing accounts of dreams, not my own or anyone else's.
I am not writing historical re-enactments of any durational literature.

I am not writing anything that anyone has requested of me or is waiting on, not a poetics essay or any other sort of essay, not a roundtable response, not interview responses, not writing prompts for younger writers, not my thoughts about critical theory or popular songs.

I am not writing a new constitution for the republic of no history.
I am not writing a will or a medical report.

I am not writing Facebook status updates. I am not writing thank-you notes or apologies. I am not writing conference papers. I am not writing book reviews. I am not writing blurbs.

I am not writing about contemporary art. I am not writing accounts of my travels. I am not writing reviews for *The New Inquiry* and not writing pieces for *Triple Canopy* and not writing anything for *Fence*. I am not writing a daily accounting of my reading, activities, and ideas. I am not writing science fiction novels about the problem of the idea of the autonomy of art and science fiction novels about the problem of a society with only one law which is consent. I am not writing stories based on

Nathaniel Hawthorne's unwritten story ideas. I am not writing online dating profiles. I am not writing anonymous communiqués. I am not writing textbooks.

I am not writing a history of these times or of past times or of any future times and not even the history of these visions which are with me all day and all of the night.

WHAT IS "NOT WRITING"?

There are years, days, hours, minutes, weeks, moments, and other measures of time spent in the production of "not writing." Not writing is working, and when not working at paid work working at unpaid work like caring for others, and when not at unpaid work like caring, caring also for a human body, and when not caring for a human body many hours, weeks, years, and other measures of time spent caring for the mind in a way like reading or learning and when not reading and learning also making things (like garments, food, plants, artworks, decorative items) and when not reading and learning and working and making and caring and worrying also politics, and when not politics also the kind of medication which is consumption, of sex mostly or drunkenness, cigarettes, drugs, passionate love affairs, cultural products, the internet also, then time spent staring into space that is not a screen, also all the time spent driving, particularly here where it is very long to get anywhere, and then to work and back, to take her to school and back, too.

There is illness and injury which has produced a great deal of not writing. There is cynicism, disappointment, political outrage, heartbreak, resentment, and realistic thinking which has produced a great deal of not writing. There is reproduction which has been like illness and injury and taken up many hours with not writing. There is being anxious or depressed which takes up many hours though not very much once there is no belief in mental health. There is trauma which is fantastic in the way it is brief and clear and also the way it lingers around and emerges unpredictably as if it will forever. Trauma is always the indirect direct producer of so much not writing. It is like a mind which has a shadow and then is the shadow and then isn't a mind or its shadow but isn't at all.

There are some hours, though not very many, on airplanes, and times with friends spent in the production of not writing. There is talking which is like writing and which produces not writing in equal measure to producing writing. There is an amount of time not writing which is not wanting to actually have to talk to humans unless it is in order to get them to have sex or in order to convince them to leave. There is sleep, which is often dreams, which is closer to writing—dreams are more like writing than not writing in that they are not intruded upon in their moments by the necessities of all the paid work, care work, social expectations, romantic love or talking to people. There is sleep which is often about gossip, architecture, and modes of civic planning and in this is closer to writing than not writing. In the dreams there is always walking around, finding walls, follies, and not getting to one place or the next but it is often those I love but whom I do not get to see very much who walk with me. There are photographs one takes, of oneself and of other people and it is in these there is the production of not writing. There is dressing and undressing, sometimes too much, particularly when things have run away, died, or one has to meet new people. There is shopping, which is a woman shopping.

There is in not writing not very much time spent on envy which is a pang, mostly, which is motivating like getting a buzz from an outlet telling one to remove one's hand from the outlet, from the power source. There is the way that the lives of others seem so often unenviable and only enviable as they are "writing" when all this time is spent not writing like right now in the not writing in which I should be dealing with bills, mail, laundry, my bedroom, months of emails from October onward even though it is now June, with my jobs, with care, with the contents of my refrigerator, with my flat tire, with the cat's litter box, with friendship, with Facebook, with my body which wants to get in the swimming pool with my body which wants to turn brown in the sun with my body which wants to drink some tea with my body which wants to do shoulder presses which wants to join a gym which wants to take a shower and get cleaned up which wants a lover which mostly wants to swim and then there is "not writing." There is envy which is also mixed with repulsion at those who do not have a long list of not writing to do.

It is easy to imagine not writing, both accidentally and intentionally. It is easy because there have been years and months and days I have thought the way to live was not writing have known what writing consisted of and have thought "I do not want to do that" and "writing steals from my loved ones" and "writing steals from my life and gives me nothing but pain and worry and what I can't have" or "writing steals from my already empty bank account" or "writing gives me ideas I do not need or want" or "writing is the manufacture of impossible desire" or writing is like literature is like the world of monsters is the production of culture is I hate culture is the world of wealthy women and of men.

A WOMAN SHOPPING

I will soon write a long, sad book called *A Woman Shopping*. It will be a book about what we are required to do and also a book about what we are hated for doing. It will be a book about envy and a book about barely visible things. This book would be a book also about the history of literature and literature's uses against women, also against literature and for it, also against shopping and for it. The flâneur is a poet is an agent free of purses, but a woman is not a woman without a strap over her shoulder or a clutch in her hand.

The back matter of the book will only say this: *If a woman has no purse, we will imagine one for her.*

These would be the chapters:

On a woman shopping
On men shopping, with and without women
On children with women as they shop
On the barely moving lips of the calculating and poor
On attempting to open doors for the elderly and in the process of this, touching their arms
On the acquiring of arms in action movies
On Daniel Defoe
On the time I saw a homeless man murdered for shoplifting
On whether it is better to want nothing or steal everything
On how many of my hours are gone now because I have had to shop
On how I wish I could shop for hours instead

There would be more: lavish descriptions of lavish descriptions of the perverse or decadently feminized marketplace, some long sentences concerning the shipping and distribution of alterity, an entire chapter about *Tender Buttons* in which each sentence is only a question. And from where did that mutton, that roast beef, that carafe come?

But who would publish this book and who, also, would shop for it? And how could it be literature if it is not coyly against literature, but sincerely against it, as it is also against ourselves?

VENGE-TEXT

I will leave no memoir, just a bitch's *Maldoror*. There's a man. He tells me he does not like the version of the story in which he is like Simon Legree who ties me down to the railroad tracks. This is because he is like Simon Legree who ties me down to the railroad tracks. He is the man who looks at the blue sky and says "Do not remember this blue sky as blue."

I look with my eyes at the blue sky and see that it is blue, then also I look with my eyes at him and make a note to not remember the blue sky as blue. I make a note, also, to remember the proclamation, by him, against the color of the sky. I make a note, also, that I will have known the sky was blue, then I will have been told to forget what I know about the sky and probably did. I make a note to doubt the legibility of any of these notes for these are notes about people who together believe a human sentence—one spoken by a man and heard by a woman—can commute the blueness of the sky itself.

That I would walk outside each day and see a blue sky would mean whatever. That so many years I have seen blue skies does not make the blue sky on that day blue.

There's an equal, independent truth that exists along with the sky itself: this is what he says against it. In this, he is like some other men: commanding. The sky can exist as a knowable color. But the commands of such men are equally persistent and knowable, too.

Despite the reality of the sky, that it is blue, a woman with any interior is trumped by a man with any exterior. Or that is what I read in the notes: even the color of the sky is stable only as long as it has a man's proof.

This is just one available story. I have so far been able to construct twenty two. I have been able to tell myself twenty two hundred stories while tied down to the railroad tracks by the lover who says he is like Simon Legree in order that he will not be in the version of the story in which he is like Simon Legree.

I suspect, like many humans in this culture, I have seen more commands of men then I have seen the sky itself. Of the two realities—the one of the sky, empirical and a color, and the one of the man who insists upon telling another person what she has seen with her own eyes of the sky is not real—I have arrived at the man's.

I have been reading about him in books: "I do not know, of all that, what was attractive about this person; but I immediately felt it was a very simple matter to love such a man."

SCIENCE FICTION

CHAPTER I

One imagines that one can escape a category by collapsing it, but if one tries to collapse the category, the roof falls on one's head. There a person is, then, having not escaped the category, but having only changed its architecture. Once it was a category with a roof, now it is a category in which everyone is buried in the rubble made of what once was a roof over their heads.

CHAPTER II

In the history of all hitherto existing societies there is fantasy and there is fantasy. The unpredictable, heaving plurality that is not really men is no fantasy. But the category of men provides the same show every day. Someone says "Would you be better if the show were a little different?" And you say *yes yes yes yes yes yes,* you are *merely bored,* you tell him, you are *weary,* you tell him, you *have seen the show so many times, but it's not really too bad, maybe just a few changes*—

But you can see some other things, like what they say is a stage is the actual heaving everything of the human everyone. It requires no separate class of actors upon it.

You watch the form of men as they act with each other in ritualized opposition to create the illusion that the actors upon the stage are in fact the scene. They've been playing at the same struggle for a long time: to keep the struggle theatrical fixes power.

But there is another, real struggle: it's not between actor and actor. It's between the actors and the stage.

TWILIGHT REVERY

Loving to disappear is not in itself *l'amour fou*. There is a controlling impulse also called "self-abolition." It can also feel warm like things burning.

And what is an addict of denial? Who does that? At first it looks like denying another or others, but it's more like an infliction of solipsism on a test subject in whatever lab. The test is on the subject more like a training but to the tester more like art. It's the total micro-expansion or macro-narrowing of pleasure. No one grows bored: what is the perversion which involves an almost graze of a non-dominant hand's second-most minor finger? Like most perversion this is a perversion with a taxonomical satisfaction: the category of thing, not thing, almost thing, of maybe thing but not quite. The same goes for acts. To do, or almost do, to begin to do but refuse, to rehearse some doing but never act, to appear to do but actually do another thing entirely—what is done also undone by that. There is vicarious doing. The thing, also vicarious: an object which exists only as it might exist to another.

The world of things so often barely perceptible. It's a condition. It can be diagnosed. To be precise, it is a condition called an entire city built on a city built on a city built on a city built on a city built on a city built on a city. It is a condition called "infinite sedimentary monument not to cities but to sediment itself." But it is a condition: that is, it is a set of unstable foundations, holes, tunnels, passageways from one strata to the next. And in the strata, not ruin, but the war before it. And every movement is a movement upward rather than the settling. What moves up?

Assume my greatest talent remains dreaming while still awake. I can talk through it. I'm being literal. You could lie in bed with me and hear for yourself. In some other era, a person like this gets a temple and whatever temple guards, protective animals, a costume and some food. Inside, it'd be a micro-state of perpetually amusing unfiltered civic liminality. Or she'd get burned.

Guess this is all just what is less about geology than cosmos.
Guess this is just the supreme whateverness of upward moving depths.

I left on the ninth day of September of that year. My name was Anne Boyer. I was unfolding under the pale of vermin. I was afraid of dying. I went into many hopeless loves. But to have whirled through the air and burst into a thousand lines? That was too intense for a perfectly quiet horse.

Suddenly I felt like a jerk.

The muscles of the legs and abdomen were half the things that were too close for me. The poets were so fond of me that they did everything they could besides beat me.

What right had they to make me suffer like the tallest building in the world?

Even this was a form of enervation. The world knew the sequel should be burned. Any famous life-size portrait only means they'll cut you. No joy, perhaps, among brutes and blockheads. The noble-souled will fail.

I drove on a highway through black clouds, sun showers, past barns and unincorporated towns. It was green there, with the crops ripening unevenly. Inside the sentence with no comma the meatpacking factories smelled less like Russia than like exile. I knew what it was like to be unpunctuated. I was ready to give up on nature, but I found a dead bat, folded as if asleep.

My daughter at that time was five years old. When she saw a neighborhood cat carrying a freshly killed baby bunny she said to me: "Anne, I can hardly stand it, how nature eats nature." It was a time when we dreamed of zombies. We dreamed of a black banty chicken who broke out of her small white house. We dreamed of an old man whose stick-limbs were swaddled, whose giant head, above the swaddling, spoke only to make anagrams out of phrases spoken around him. At the top of a parking garage, I stood next to him and stared at a river. The river was swollen and carrying off trash and broken trees.

But poems weren't written in any language I wanted to read. I thought I could maintain modesty writing prose. I wanted furniture that had been burned to resemble furniture that had been burned. This is just one view of that microscopic tragedy: the Sudanese women wore yellow head wraps and walked through drifts of snow. The battery was weak there. The alarm chirped.

The country forcing language to speak straight was very different from my own. Because I had that rustic way of going abstract I feared for myself and all verbal orgies. I feared for the fact that things were out of order. I feared for my jaw and tongue. It was eighteen degrees at ten o'clock, and we had no heat. The sign in the entry hall of The Kingman, where I then lived, said,

THE HEAT S ON.

Another tenant wrote on that sign,

IF IT IS I HAVE AN FELT IT YET.

I filled up the bathtub with water boiled on the stove, and the windows went opaque with steam. The coffee went cold in a minute. My daughter and I put all the blankets and clothes we owned over us. I decided I would be a poet so that I could complain publicly of this.

Around that time my daughter and I had this exchange:

Anne, imagine if the world had nothing in it.

Do you mean nothing at all—just darkness—or a world without objects?

I mean a world without things: no houses, chairs, or cars. A world with only people and trees and dirt.

What do you think would happen?

People would make things. We would make things with trees and dirt.

In August all the fish in the Aquarium of the Americas died At that time I wanted to be nice like a word in a dictionary. I was anonymous, or trying to be. I lost my head. I fell in love with everyone. Love was a figure of speech.

When the German girl died, Charlemagne had her embalmed and put her corpse in his bed. He then fell in love with the corpse. A bishop, suspecting enchantment, found a ring under the corpse's tongue. When the bishop removed the ring from the corpse and put it in his pocket, Charlemagne lost interest in the corpse and fell in love with the Bishop. The Bishop threw the ring in Lake Constance. Charlemagne fell in love with the lake.

It was the month of November of that year, and I had only been to the ocean twice and once it was the sea. I was afraid of nothing.

"It only appears to be nothing," the man who was then my lover told me.

The third time, I saw a seal. The beaches were almost black, and a mist rose, and the rocks towered, and I found some smooth stones and a few broken abalone shells and a piece of sea glass. I sat on a giant driftwood log and remembered what I read in the hotel: "Never turn your back to the tide."

The crows must have known what was up, for that year there were hordes of them, each one of them the size of a cat. They took over empty trees so that the empty trees were not empty, but looked as if they were made of leaves of feathers and wings. *If God had let me live just five years longer, I'd have been a writer,* but a place with such vastness had no audience but itself. And what did I like about myself?

I liked the philosophers, except when they bored me.

In the laboratory, survival borrowed the form of divination. Then I dreamed, wrote stories, acquired information, called my fellows to take action, fetishized parts for wholes, watched the pornography of the common disaster, submitted the spectacle of my humanity to humanity for entertainment. There were so many takes just to capture one frame of suffering! Who was not comfortable, finally, to become like a mime?

In November of the next year I was in the blackness of the elements and manifesting the gloomiest reserve. I thought there needed to be trap doors, strings of cans, a net rigged up to four trees, motion sensing lights, protective hounds. I thought it was meant to be praise. I was often false to this knowledge, in idolatries of particular objects, or impatient longings for happiness. I assumed that language was a symptom of disease. I assumed I had no one to speak to. I knew there were at least two rules: 1. To speak. 2. To not speak. Also 3. To almost speak. 4. To stand ready to speak, but with shut lips. 5. To refuse all terms. Then I knew there were many more rules, but I did not know them all.

I was too sad to slug in the face. I was stoned and inconsolable. I was a weary rocket engineer looking at the twisted remains of a bad shot-defined astronautics. I wanted to be addendum free.

Two squirrels, either mating or fighting, grabbed at each others necks with teeth. It was some economy of attention, the consumer who never noticed that she had paid enough. And the clichés that killed you were the clichés of note. These were the most common means of suffering, and of them I would ask, "Who eats in a cage? Or with a caged mouth?"

In the car I heard something, and the man who was then my lover said THAT WAS PROBABLY A MOCKINGBIRD—but it sounded like something else. I then learned that the point of those birds was to sound like something else.

"a private passage on melancholy from around that time"

Having no interest in realism suddenly I had an interest in realism, if not exactly realism, representation, if not representation only a skilled represen-tation, or if not any of this my interest was in skill, in acquiring skill, in learning to do things and how things are done and what is the reason for doing them.

What I was really interested in was a moat and a large stone wall and a hair-triggered army and unreliable aides and a tower, perhaps, and a few vials of quick- or slow-acting poison, and a hallucination of encroaching enemies, and the frivolity of court. And interested in this, suddenly I was interested in the unguarded and bucolic: in Kansas, a white bull alone by a farm pond on a golden plain, a girl gluing, and color charts.

But I was not interested. Some in those days were sick with the world, some were sick from lack of it, and they were two opposite sicknesses and also sometimes two simultaneous sicknesses, and certainly two sicknesses requir-ing two or more cures.

Things changed and soon enough all I wanted to know is how to draw a don-key. Some people knit coral reefs. Once I painted clear acrylic gel over pho-tocopies of stills and airplanes and then at midnight soaked the photocopies in water and rubbed the paper off. I was happy to have remembered to write about this, so that I could repeat the act later. I spilled coffee on the outside of my car. I wanted in my melancholy to carve a stamp of a bird. I did laundry. I drew a hand: it looked like a claw.

I said that maybe everyone I knew was embarrassed by me. I went on being embarrassing. There were at least two kinds of people: those who loathed the world and found themselves trapped in the terribleness of it and those who loathed themselves as foil to the world. I didn't consider it stupid to take notes on this.

The man who was then my lover would dream of one me (Anne Boyer) protecting another me (Anne Boyer). But these were two different Anne Boyers, one like a cop, the other writing her name at a table. I thought to want regard was to want scorpions in your shower. I thought to speak was to ask for a muzzle. I thought to feel or to show you feel was to ask a sadist to make you flail. I thought to have a name was to have oneself abstracted and abstracted again into many bodies, some actual and corporeal or some ghostly or whiffs or some so strange, so far from you, they might as well be astral. I thought to have a name was to become an object. I thought I was a charlatan. I was mistaken. I was not a charlatan, I was a search term.

Synesthesia was not a dream, but close, and during the night the cell phone ring was like facets on diamonds. My daughter, who was then six, said "I am the queen of fall, and metal is my enemy." She told me during that time how the queen controlled the weather with smells as a queen bee protected her hive.

I wrote down this quotation but could not remember its source: "How many a poor Hazlitt must wander on God's verdant earth, like the Unblest on burning deserts; passionately dig wells, and draw up only the dry quicksand; believe that he is seeking Truth, yet only wrestle among endless Sophisms, doing desperate battle as with spectre-hosts; and die and make no sign!" In the parking lot of The Franklin Court, where I then lived, a hawk twisted its head behind itself, and stared at me.

It was a time of many car troubles, so I waited for tow trucks and saw a squirrel with a marble in her mouth. It was a time of many money troubles, so I wrote about money or wanted to.

I thought I would write about money and then those who did not yet write about money would soon write about money

What was I, poor? I spent seventy-three cents on a cookie for my daughter. I got a fifty-dollar Wal-Mart gift card in the mail. I sold a painting of a lamb for three hundred and eighty-five dollars.

During this time I invented many quotations about money:

It is right for MONEY *to be indistinguishable from what is foreseen and not yet formulated.* —René Char

MONEY *never had a beginning. Always, until the moment of its stopping, it was constantly there.* —Boris Pasternak

Be MONEY *like the universe!* —Fernando Pessoa

Such an act of judgment, distinguishing between Chance and Providence, deserves, surely, to be called MONEY. —W. H. Auden

Now so many people write about money that it is very easy, like writing about love. But in those days if you couldn't write about what you had left, you couldn't write about anything. I thought how uncomfortable it would be if I wrote about money. I thought about this a lot.

Things were great after that. They really got better. I wrote words in great paragraphs. There were great acorns. I had a great toothache. There was the great noise of the great leaving geese.

But I had been striking against geography for a very long time. Or rather, the systems I believed would end my loneliness amplified it, though I managed most days to feign delight in the wide expanses and simple clothing styles of my native land. These systems that amplified my loneliness included cars, airplanes, computers, and telephones. These systems included universities, literary presses, major American cities, the U. S. mail, and several private mail carriers including U. P. S. and Federal Express.

All my breathing apparatus rejected the air around me as not fit for breath, and storms turned streets into rivers. There was a city I didn't always remember, and then once in it, I recalled it like all cities are recalled by birds.

There were gas lamps. There were dead sows full of living birds. I thought about the poet Marcia Nardi who wrote "as if there were no connection between my being stuck at the ribbon counter in Woolworth's for eight hours a day at minimum hourly wage, and my inability to function as a poet." I was melancholy and wrote defenses of my melancholy. I totally forgot to shop.

The anesthetizing influence of habit having ceased, I would begin to have thoughts, and feelings, and they were such sad things.

I wrote complicated sentences and cursed the fantasy of war. What was imagined was that which was found &/or fleshed &/or animated in the interior & that which abided by the interior's logic rather than the material necessities of everything else—not a subjectivity composed of sentiments and sensations, but a subjectivity composed of acts and figures.

Maybe this was a halfway subjectivity or a connective one, what animated the forms of the material as they become the immaterial forms in the mind. When something was then imagined, it was experienced—with sensations and sentiments vivid as any other. Maybe any distrust of the imagination was a distrust of feeling and arose when one was unable to parse interior experiences (acts and figures) from interior responses (emotion and sensation) to those experiences.

My visions and dreams and flights of fancy were no more sentimental or sensational in themselves than events and interactions of the material world. Insofar as the imagination might be more cunning at provoking strong feelings it did not mean that the imagination was itself not inextricable from feeling. Dreams were the highest order of my experience. Then they were what I imagined was at best an entertaining fiction or sometimes a profitable product.

I wanted to keep unfashionable experience alive.

And there was, I thought, a reasonably justifiable distinction between she who was captivated by the imagination and she who was captivated by the world.

But a vision was not an event. What remained? Just a sorry state of fumy halls, dreams in a gas of acetone and ammonia doused in a floral bouquet: the Colonial Gardens, where I then lived, on the night of the chemical spill.

A few months before the chemical spill I had a Stockholm feeling. I proposed bans on Monumental Architectures, Expertise, and Tones of Authority. I wrote a recipe for a chocolate cake you can bake when you own only one small round pan. I include this here:

A chocolate cake for when you own only one small round pan

One stick of butter
3.5-ounce bar of very dark chocolate
$\frac{1}{2}$ cup of cocoa
$\frac{3}{4}$ cup of flour
$\frac{1}{2}$ teaspoon salt
$\frac{1}{2}$ teaspoon baking soda
$\frac{3}{4}$ teaspoon baking powder
2 eggs
$\frac{3}{4}$ cup sugar
1 tablespoon good vanilla
$\frac{1}{2}$ cup plain yogurt

Preheat oven to 350° & prepare your one small round cake pan (I use butter and flour). Melt chocolate, cocoa & butter over low heat. Sift dry things in one bowl. Whisk eggs, sugar & vanilla in the other. Add melted things. Whisk. Add dry things. Whisk. Add yogurt. Stir. Put in cake pan, where it just fits. Bake 20 minutes or until done. Slice in half when cool & frost in two layers with vanilla butter cream.

This was a very good cake, and we ate it all.

These were the years that I believed it was still possible to move in cars down streets while socked-in-the-gut about the terror hidden in the history of objects, in the stores full of objects, in the homes, also, full of objects. I believed that leaving most of the furniture for the neighbors made room in the bed of the truck for my books, but having left all I had so I could keep for myself what I had tried so hard to gather, my books were soon ruined by rain. I was deprived of objects and the world of objects, but because of this I was in thrall to such boring things, like finding chairs by dumpsters, and in this I was reminded exactly of my resentment of you.

But what you really asked was another question: is it possible to write about objects—the way things look and feel, the garments on bodies and in furniture in the gardens and in the rooms without somehow also provoking a desire to acquire more things, or even if one writes about making things is it possible to write about making things without also provoking desire for them?

A thin and leggy kit squatted in front of the car that I had stopped to watch him. He shit on the asphalt, walked away, proceeded to be deranged or leisurely in the grass of the yard. He stared at me when I rolled down the window to talk to him. He was half-curious at birds in a tree, but not curious enough to attempt to eat them. On the next block a dove squatted in front of the car so that I could run her over. I had no choice and she blinked and did not move and was not hit by my tire. When the car behind me ran over her, I could see in the rear view mirror her panic and that before she died she flew up against the car only slightly.

It was in September I totally fucked with chronology. I thought memoirs were written by property owners. I was about to fall in love with younger men. When I went back to work at my former employer, offices had been established inside of elevators, and I was asked by my boss "Well do you want to go to the dinner because that would make it 102? Too many, don't you think?" His daughter was dressed as a witch. I taught her to say *Maximus.*

In auditoriums, cheerleaders practiced their dances, different squads in different colors with different choreography dancing to the same song. Outside, climate change had caused the environment to become a disaster movie called "Ice Age." This meant if you stepped off the veranda you would be engulfed by an icy, hard-driving flood, and there would be a soundtrack and voiceover for this.

I was at university in China. There was large, colorful glass dripping or falling in shards from ceilings above stairwells and also the walls. The Chinese university decided to blow up their own duck pond, and in one hour I saw both a pond full of duck and the ruins of a pond full of ducks, the feathers on the not-yet-dead ducks singed, them gasping and lurching all around me. After the pond exploded I befriended an American boy skilled in the ways of murdering young spies so as to steal their magic shoes. I turned my magic shoes into red sneakers, and upon visiting the English department, learned with horror that my office held no bed. I installed my bed and clothes into a broom closet without a lock. I watched with some fascination as the literary tourists came to see the office of Anne Boyer. My friend took me to a wedding, then, with a theme of middle-aged men marrying young girls.

All the poet houses were made of glass, so when the storm came from Darfur, their houses were half-wrecked and one could see big holes. I decided it was okay to fly again, so got in my little black airplane and tried to decide if I wanted to go to Mexico, France, New York City, or Pennsylvania, all within easy reach. Then I decided to land the plane in a field, got a black bike, abandoned the bike, walked to a therapist's office (tucked in the back of a five and dime) and though I was around for my appointment, missed it (it was at 1:30) yet at 6:00 insisted (cried) and met the therapist and told him I'd abandoned my plane. He told me to get a black car.

I was at the edge of cites. I was at the edge of economies. In those days some even accused me of googling my dreams.

I ignored the ordinary digital manners of those times.

These were the days when they made a great mistake about me. I felt an acute self-consciousness and could not remove the vanguard's weaknesses to relieve these spasms. I knew nothing of the long, heavy claws of pardon. The air was sick hot. The great roving gang of neighborhood toms hid out until nightfall, then wailed in chorus. I had once had morning glories. I had once had *Marvels of Peru*. I did not stand, free from desire. And somewhere between the chemical fluorescence and the primeval murk, people tried to help me. I threw up my hands.

I did once bite the enemy's guns, warding off another by pushing them ever on. I wanted to write the word as my loved ones had wished it of me. I wanted to write the words of the restive me, sitting motionless for a year. But I had never been a beauty. I gave myself to mount. I knew all these moods and videotaped everything. It was on that day that we heard the firing of the heavy guns.

The story went on, for the most part, with a kind of lovely unease, spending days in bed, claiming I was a nun, painting abstracted farm scenes. Despite the preferences of the poets of my generation I did not quote from the lyrics of the popular music of the time. I could not move from the center of the space, so I said to everyone, as if I meant it, "We will leave it here."

It has kind of killed me to tell you about this. The man who had been my lover sat on the divan making anagrams out of Shakespeare's sonnets. I was nervous about lineage and public assistance. I was half-cool but not entirely. Several men declared publicly that they would destroy me. Several men declared privately that they would destroy me. I did not believe in the abstract lyric. There had been cartoons. We were on lists.

Such worries I only sometimes let myself have. What had happened to me was a hybrid of chance and agency, and though I should have gone swimming, I took a nap. It was December, and I looked kind of pale and sick because I had diffused the horror by rubbing against things. Then the ice melted, the bright sun shone, and I remembered garages and the people who owned them. I dreamed of a used car lot and a rifle. I envied those who walked on four feet. I had a problem with capital letters. I admitted to the debt. These were the days I had to go do dim things in government offices, and believed, once again, in the danger of aspirations.

I was poor, I was solitary, and I undertook to devote myself to literature in a community in which the interest in literature was as yet of the smallest. I believed that autodidacts were here to teach decency. I believed I'd lost my front. I kept checking the social fabric for the hole I'd burned. I dreamed someone had written a sign: ANNE SAYS SHE WILL NEVER RETURN A CALL. I noted that the qualia of my consciousness were like redness or pain. I was certain there were elements of experience about which one could never write. Instead I went to the American states of Georgia, California, Nebraska, Colorado, Pennsylvania, New York, Oregon, Maine, Illinois, Texas, North Carolina, Kansas, Iowa, and Missouri. I believed that if one came to poetry for solace one was fucked. I believed things would go on like this.

I then created a deep system for the perpetuation and proliferation of denial, and that system had many nodes, and in these nodes there were rubrics for evaluation, and as one node sensed that the system was feeding power to another node, it flared and insisted that I feed power to it. I wrote so many signs saying ANNE ANSWER YOUR EMAILS but never could do just that. But I had to end this story somewhere. I chose that moment when I fell in love. You see I was a man who enjoyed the grandeur of buildings. You see I was a woman who took notes. Everyone was very kind and wanted to help, but in order to be clear about it, I will tell the story like this: it appears that she refused the ladder, but in truth she refused the rope.

Did I explain that those days were the days when the people wrote on machines that connected to machines that connected to machines that connected to people who wrote on machines?

Those were the days when we believed in information.

And I was a person in those days, but I did not believe in information. I liked to imagine the interfaces that would make the public private and make the private okay.

Privacy was not an effect, exactly, of confession, which in those days was buying stock in the public company. Those were the days of crude luxury and genteel sorrow. Those were the days I loved to delete.

There is no such thing, really, as the public ever again. We fractured into temperate and intemperate zones and small service colonies and into villages surrounded by walls of inoperative cars. Now we can barely remember what once formed us, and the last and first thing any of us thinks about is poetry.

I did what I could. I was so lonely. I loved you. I wrote many small books using methods and forms popular and unpopular with my contemporaries. Among these books was a book of my terrors, a book of my dreams, a book of imagined things, and a book about the rabbits in the yard. I wrote a book for computers with voices. I wrote a book based on euphonious sounds. I wrote a book that was a universal novel. I wrote a book for an avant-garde collective. I wrote a book of traumatic facts. I had written only one book before that time, but at last I put the point of my life to immediate use. I wrote this memoir that you are reading, then I wrote a book that was a history of the future in advance of itself. I wrote a book that was the story of a prostitute who walked the streets of Google earth. I am now finishing a book: it is called "the innocent question" or it is called "garments against women" or it is called "this champion: life."

Rousseau tells the story of "a little girl who learnt to write before she could read, and she began to write with her needle. To begin with, she would write nothing but O's; she was always making O's, large and small, of all kinds and one within another, but always drawn backwards."

Rousseau believed the O's to be O's, but every O could have been, also, every letter and every word for the little girl: each O also an opening, a planet, a ring, a word, a query, a grammar. One O could be an eye, another a mouth, another a bruise, another a calculation.

These sentences made of O's, written with the girl's needle, might have read:

"I understand the proximate shape of the fountain"
"Apples are smaller than the sun"
"My mother"

or—in the case of the O's inside the other O's—"In nothing, we might find a few things, also nothing." Rousseau says the little girl quit: "like another Minerva she flung away her pen and declined to make any more O's."

Rousseau believed this is because the girl saw how unattractive she looked while writing. But as someone wrote in the margins of one of my books:

"ROUSSEAU KNOWS NOTHING ABOUT OTHER PEOPLE"

Rousseau's little girl saw herself in the mirror, writing, but she did not quit writing because she could not tolerate a reflection of her own unloveliness.

The little girl quit writing because what she saw in the mirror was the message she had written to herself in code.

Her language of O's was written backwards: in this, it was most accurately read in the mirror in which she also saw herself. In the mirror was literature as a set of practical instructions, including this one: "Throw down the-pen-that-is-your-needle and refuse to write again."

Rousseau's little girl threw her needle down because of what she had taught herself, and after that, Rousseau said she became almost an entirely different person. After that, she was only persuaded to write again in order to mark what was hers.

The little girl in Rousseau needed only to write down her own name now: she had written, already, her revolutionary letters in the code of O's.

the walserian monument. a walserian wedding.
walserian joie de vivre. a walserian ship at not-
sail. the maybe floating of a walserian upon

their back inside a possible stream. walserian
#motto YSRWTLO ("you shouldn't really
want to live once"). a clerk's antinomy.

antinomian clerk. count-down (o).
after-math (o). walserian motherhood. citizen's
fog. professional avoidant. "civicious." plan air.

*

to go to work and work all day and go home
to sleep to get up the next day to go to work
and then to think "that was walseresque"

*

walserian pedagogy. "do not look or use
your hands." sancho panza as she-devil. the
subsubsubcategories of a whatever yes.

a catalogue of whales that is a catalogue
of whale bones inside a catalogue of garments
against women that could never be a novel itself.

NOTES AND ACKNOWLEDGMENTS

"The Animal Model of Inescapable Shock" first appeared in *The New Inquiry*. The poem "Garments Against Women" first appeared in *Critical Quarterly*. Maynard Shelley's *The Strategies and Tactics of Happiness Volume 1: Background* is out of print. The "Charlie" mentioned here, who made the "less typing" drawing, is the artist Charlie Mylie. "A man who falls straight into bed night after night, and ceases to live until the morning when he wakes and rises, will surely never dream of making, I don't say great discoveries, but even minor observations about sleep. He scarcely knows that he is asleep" is a quote from Marcel Proust. "Not Writing" was written in the summer of 2012 in response to a prompt from Coda Wei. One can read more from Marcia Nardi, whose letters William Carlos Williams turned, without her permission, into the Cress letters of *Paterson*, in *The Last Word: Letters Between Marcia Nardi and William Carlos Williams*, edited by Elizabeth Murrie O'Neil, and published by the University of Iowa Press in 1994. "I like the philosophers, except when they bore me" is a line from *Paul Gauguin's Intimate Journals*. It continues, "I like women too, when they are fat and vicious." "Strike Against Geography" is a phrase of the composer and writer Jace Clayton. I first read about Charlemagne and the servant girl in Italo Calvino's *Six Memos for the Next Millennium*. "How many a poor Hazlitt must wander on God's verdant earth . . ." can now be located: it's from Thomas Carlyle's essay on Lord Byron. "He was poor, he was solitary, and he undertook to devote himself to literature in a community in which the interest in literature was as yet of the smallest" is how Henry James described Nathaniel Hawthorne. Edith Thomas, in *The Women Incendiaries*, available in English translation from Haymarket Books, wrote about the rumor that during the commune, proletarian women roamed the streets of Paris like witches, with kerosene and torches, marking what they wished to be destroyed with BPB—*Bon*

Pour Brûler (good for burning). The story of the little girl who wrote only in O's is found in the *Emile and Sophie* chapter of Rousseau's *Emile*. In Robert Walser's *Jakob Von Guten*, you can read this sentence: "I shall be a charming, utterly spherical zero."

I thank Robert J. Baumann, Alex Savage, and Cara Lefebvre for their friendship and support during the Colonial Gardens years. It was with them, in the strip malls and near the dumpsters, at Karaoke night at the Long Branch Saloon or waking to the speakers of the used car lot, that the substance of this book was formed. I also thank Aaron Kunin for letting me think about happiness with him in the late spring of 2009, Dana Ward and Stephanie Young for convincing me to stop sewing in October of 2010, and Jasper Bernes, who has always been there to read when I've been around to write. I also thank my daughter, Hazel, who has allowed me the possibility of a literature that is not against us and to whom I dedicate this book.

ABOUT THE AUTHOR

ANNE BOYER is a poet who lives in Kansas.

AHSAHTA PRESS

SAWTOOTH POETRY PRIZE SERIES

AHSAHTA PRESS

NEW SERIES

This book is set in Apollo MT type
with DIN Light titles
by Ahsahta Press at Boise State University.
Cover design by Quemadura.
Book design by Janet Holmes.

AHSAHTA PRESS

2015

JANET HOLMES, DIRECTOR

ADRIAN KIEN, ASSISTANT DIRECTOR

DENISE BICKFORD

KATIE FULLER

LAURA ROGHAAR

ELIZABETH SMITH

KERRI WEBSTER